CORONAVIRUS

Let's Talk About Sex During a Pandemic

Made Simple

Dr. Rosie Milligan

Copyright © 2020 by Dr. Rosie Milligan
Los Angeles, California
All rights reserved
Printed and Bound in the United States of America

Published and Distributed by
Professional Publishing House LLC
1425 W. Manchester Ave. Ste. B
Los Angeles, California 90047
323-750-3592
Email: professionalpublishinghouse@yahoo.com
www.Professionalpublishinghouse.com

Cover design: TWA Solutions
First Printing: April 2020
978-1-7328982-2-6
10987654321

No part of this book may be reproduced, stored in a retrieval system or transmitted in any form or by any means without the prior written permission of the publisher—except by a reviewer who may quote brief passages in a review to be printed in a newspaper, magazine or journal.

For inquiries contact the author at drrosie@aol.com

Acknowledgments

Firstly, I want to thank God for my life and for aiding in the working of my faith in Him to be able to do all the things that I have done successfully.

To my late father, Simon Hunter, who instilled in me to fear nothing and this too shall pass. It's because of his teachings that I can stand in times of adversities.

To my children, who, because of them being good children, afforded me to do me without worrying about them.

To my family who has been my cheerleaders—they think I can walk through brick walls—and I have attempted to do so.

To my friend, Don Spears, thank you for reminding me that I have an obligation to address the sex issues during these troubled times. Don and I conducted relationship seminars nationwide back in the nineties. I learned a lot on Black male/female relationship from a male's point of view from Don's book, *In Search of Goodpussy: Living Without Love*. This book was a #1 national best-seller. I laugh out loud even now when I think how people would buy Don's book and remove the front cover. They didn't want people to know they were reading about sex. Don Spears is a writer who has always been ahead of his time.

To my friends who have supported me in every endeavor.

About the Author

Dr. Rosie Milligan, a woman who knows no limits, is a registered nurse, critically-acclaimed author, one of Los Angeles's renowned financial gurus, a seasoned senior estate planner, business and credit consultant, and a radio host who holds a Ph.D. in Business Administration. She has always been an achiever. She is sought after nationwide for her business and financial coaching services. Every career or business she's been involved in has included helping other people accomplish their life's dream. Her motto, "Erase 'NO,' Step Over 'CAN'T,' and Move Forward With LIFE," has been a motivating influence for hundreds to whom she has been a mentor and role model.

Dr. Milligan is the most versatile speaker on the circuit today and is sought-after by religious organizations of all denominations, as well as corporate and social groups. An author of twenty-six books, she lectures nationally on economic empowerment, wealth legacy building, and male/female relationships. An expert in the publishing industry, with thirty years of experience, she owns and operates the largest and fastest-growing, independent, African American, woman-owned publishing house in the nation, Professional Publishing House LLC, where she has published more than three hundred titles. Many authors she has published and nurtured were signed by mainstream publishers and have taken their places on numerous best-seller lists across the country. Her books, *Satisfying The Black Man Sexually Made Simple, Satisfying The Black Woman Sexually Made Simple, Why Black Men Choose White Women,* and *Nigger, Please*, raised eyebrows across the county. She is the most provocative and thought-provoking writer of the century. Her latest book, *Dr. Rosie: Having Her Say* is a must-read.

A successful, motivational speaker and trainer, Dr. Milligan has appeared on numerous national television and radio talk shows and she is a regular guest on Stevie Wonder's KJLH Radio. She is also the host of a weekly live Internet talk show, EXPRESS YOURSELF HOUR, and she is the founder and director of Black Writers on Tour. Visit Drrosie.com for a list of book titles.

For Books by Dr. Rosie Milligan, see page 27.

Table of Contents

Preface 13

Chapter 1

    Men and Sex During a Crisis 17

Chapter 2

    Women and Sex During a Crisis 21

Chapter 3

    Sex and Concerns about Our Children 25

Conclusion 27

PREFACE

Facing the Coronavirus, and as we talk about the importance of social distancing, wearing facial masks and gloves, we must discuss intimacy and sex during this critical time.

Except for money, sex is the only factor in our civilized society that people permit themselves to indulge in at the risk of losing their jobs or causing harm to themselves and their families—all for a few, brief orgasmic thrills. It is the only factor that can cause a community-wide, citywide, nationwide, or international calamity. And just think, all it entails is two people consenting to have sex. However, if you do it in a manner in which people say is wrong, they will destroy you! Sex is a dominating factor in our lives. It is a moving force that keeps us going, and most of us will admit that. Sex, that obscure and yet paradoxically, mundane biological necessity, dominates us all in one way or another.

The emergence of rape, pornography, and incest is related to psycho-sexual problems. The most sought-after experience by humans, after eating, is SEX, and to continuously keep it in the closet will undoubtedly cause serious problems for future generations.

We must admit that many are sex addicts, and some are not sexually fulfilled by their spouse/partner and are having extra sexual affairs, which keeps their marriage/relationship intact.

Social distancing and government-ordered shutdown are requiring men to stay home with their wives and families while businesses are closed and jobs are laying people off due to the Coronavirus. What is a man to do when his joy, happiness, and sexual release comes from outside of his home? The frustration from this dilemma will cause havoc due to a man's frustration of being isolated at home and missing the one he wants to be with during troubled times.

Coronavirus: Let's Talk About Sex During a Pandemic

Women accustomed to their husband/partner being away from home most of the time are accustomed to chit-chatting with her friends and spending time with her children. Now enters the intruder—her husband/partner. She finds it difficult to adjust to having him home. And he does not want to be at home. This will bring about a strain on the relationship if there is no intervention. Let's talk about SEX!

CHAPTER 1

Men and Sex During a Crisis

When men face a crisis, they look for a mental escape, be it alcohol, drugs or sex. They sometimes take dangerous chances to satisfy that need for escape. When they want sex, it's not about love, it's about sex.

Sex Men Have
Lost their lives for it
Lost their jobs for it
Left their wives for it
Left their children for it
Left school for it
Gone A.W.O.L. from the military for it
All for a little piece of real estate with
grass growing on it.

Dr. Rosie Milligan

It should be of concern that hookers are no longer on the streets and strip clubs are closed due to the Coronavirus. What will these men do? How will they satisfy their sexual needs?

Men who are accustomed to having sex with their wives only now and then prior to the Coronavirus, and who now want to have sex frequently, they will probably have a problem with their wives with their new sexual appetite.

For peace sake, men, you might have to get used to practicing masturbation and provide more intimacy for a happier marriage.

Some people are not aware if they are a carrier of the Coronavirus, so you should curtail your sexual appetite. The Coronavirus is quite different from the HIV/AIDS virus, whereby you could use a condom for protection.

Men, who have been slipping and dipping, consider a sexual fast. This is not the time to be selfish. Think of those you are in contact with during the Coronavirus pandemic—consider your wife, children, family member, and friends. It's a time and a season for all things and this is the time to make your sexual thirst subject to your command.

For those of you who feel as though, you cannot survive without a biological release, and this feeling is causing turbulence in your life, I suggest you read the section on "Telephone Sex" in chapter eleven in my book, *Satisfying The Black Woman Sexually Made Simple*.

CHAPTER 2

Women and Sex During a Crisis

During a crisis, women are more concerned about feeling secure. They want more intimacy than sex. They want to feel loved and protected by their husbands/partners.

You want to have good communication with your spouse/partner. They need to know what you are feeling during these critical times. Men do not let your fears make you seclude yourself from your family. You need to assure your wife/partner that she is important to you and tell her that you appreciate her.

Men, if you have been away from the house most of the time due to your job, travel work, etc., remember, your wife/partner has been accustomed to your absence. So, work your way back into the life of your wife/partner and family gradually. Don't expect her to readily adjust to the new routine of having you home—this is new for both of you, so be patient.

Women, you need to make time for your husband/partner now that he is home during the Coronavirus Pandemic. Let your friend, whom you talk to frequently, know that your husband is home most of the time and that you will have to limit the time and frequency of your conversations—friends will understand and, if not, oh well.

Ask your husband/partner what he would like to do during this shutdown period. Find things to do that you, your husband/partner and children can do together.

Remember, it's not easy having a man at home who has been absent for years. It's going to be difficult living with a man who is trying to hide his fears and uncertainties through sex without intimacy. It is important to know that sometime men do not

Coronavirus: Let's Talk About Sex During a Pandemic

want to make love, they just want to have sex—sex is like an unwind, a tranquilizer for men—they are not into pleasing you, it's all about themselves. Get over it, men are just that way. I would suggest to men to be honest with your wife, if it is just a quickie that you are in the mood for let her know, because she may not want to have sex with you at all and is going along to get along. So don't have your wife packing for a long trip if you just want to go around the corner.

A lack of money and bedroom turmoil has been noted as two of the leading causes of dissention in a marriage/relationship. These challenging times have ushered in frustration from both—a lack of money and bedroom turmoil. And with these two occurrences, we are witnessing an increase in domestic violence. If the stress from it all is becoming overwhelming, do not hesitate to seek mental health assistance. You can get through this.

CHAPTER 3

Sex and Concerns about Our Children

During the Coronavirus Pandemic, many school children are at home alone while some parents are at work. Do not allow your children to have their friends or relatives to come over when you are away, because you do not know whether they practice safety at home.

If you have not talked to your children about sex, it's time that you do so. You should teach them the dos and don'ts about touching certain parts of their body. Many children experience molestation by friends, relatives or a parent/boyfriend in their homes when the parent(s) was not at home. It is your responsibility to let them know what touching or activity they must share with you.

Teach your teens about sex. Let them know that having an erection is normal and that they do not have to do anything about an erection and that too will pass. Tell your children that their brother/sister/father/mother should not touch them on certain body parts.

I am concerned about the molestation of children during the school closure due to the Coronavirus. Educate and stay safe.

CONCLUSION

The Coronavirus Pandemic has brought on a new experience for all of us. It has ushered in a new norm for us. Let's face this new way of living and know that things will be forever changed.

We will get through this together. I am so happy to see how those who have means are stepping up to the plate to help those who have not.

Embrace this new way of life and be safe. And when it comes to sex, check yourself before you wreck yourself. Sexual starvation will not kill you, but having sex with the wrong person and at the wrong time can cause your demise. THINK.

Books by Dr. Rosie Milligan

*Coronavirus: Let's Talk About Sex
During A Pandemic Made Simple*

*Coronavirus: Lessons Learned From the Shutdown
That You Should Incorporate Going Forward*

Dr. Rosie: Having Her Say

Satisfying The Black Man Sexually Made Simple

*Satisfying The Black Woman
Sexually Made Simple*

Why Black Men Choose White Women

Starting a Business Made Simple

What You Need to Know Before Starting a Business

Getting Out of Debt Made Simple

What You Need To Know Before You Get Hitched

Departing This Life Preparations

Creating A New You In Six Weeks Made Simple

Understanding Credit Made Simple

Creating a Budget Made Simple

Milliganisms: "Motional Quotations" and "How Comes"

How to Write a Book Made Simple

Nuts and Bolts For The New Author And The New Publisher Made Simple

ABC's On How To Prepare Your Manuscript

ABC's For Starting And Managing Your Own Publishing Company Made Simple

Developing A Marketing Plan For Your Book Made Simple

Negroes, Colored People, Blacks and African Americans in America

Nigger, Please.

Black America Faces Economic Crisis

African American Resource Guide

Steps to Success (Co-authored with L C Green)

Dynamic Principles of Financial Control
(Co-authored with LC Green)

www.ingramcontent.com/pod-product-compliance
Lightning Source LLC
Chambersburg PA
CBHW060345080526
44584CB00013B/923